This book is dedicated to
Monsignor Andreatti
with happy memories of a special
Mamma, Nonna and Papa,
all born in 1911.

Love Finse

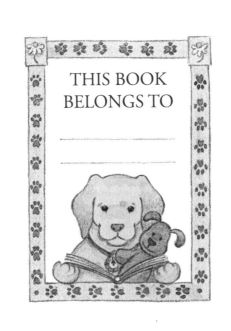

THIS BOOK
BELONGS TO

_____

_____

"Finse Explores Italy"

The right of Karine Hagen to be identified as the author
and Suzy-Jane Tanner to be identified as the illustrator
of this work has been asserted by them in accordance
with the Copyright Designs and Patents Act 1988.

First published by Viking Cruises
83 Wimbledon Park Side, London, SW19 5LP

ISBN 978-1-909968-10-3

www.finse.me

Produced by Colophon Digital Projects Ltd,
Old Isleworth, TW7 6RJ, United Kingdom
Printed in China.

FINSE
EXPLORES ITALY

Karine Hagen
Suzy-Jane Tanner

FINSE EXPLORES ITALY

LOVENIA

CROATIA

BOSNIA & HERZEGOVINA

MONTENEGRO

Ancona

Adriatic Sea

Naples

I remember Grandpup Percy telling us how every summer, his Great Great Grandpup Dunsmere set out from my puppyhood home, Highclere Castle, in his Rolls Royce to explore the Italian Riviera.

I decided I would explore Italy too!

I arrived in Genoa and met my dogfriend Biagio.

He showed me the historic medieval quarter of the city and told me about famous people who had been born there, including the explorer Christopher Columbus and violinist Niccolò Paganini.

The city of Milan is famous for elegant fashion design. The term millinery for hat making is derived from the name Milan.

Opera was born in Italy in 1598. La Scala opera house in the city is one of the greatest in the world.

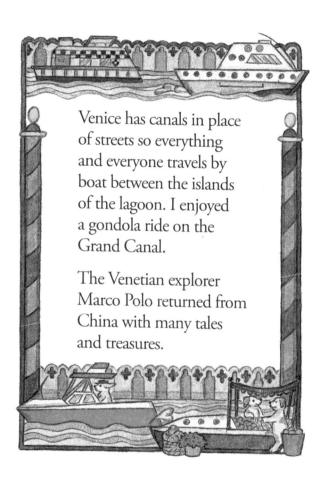

Venice has canals in place of streets so everything and everyone travels by boat between the islands of the lagoon. I enjoyed a gondola ride on the Grand Canal.

The Venetian explorer Marco Polo returned from China with many tales and treasures.

11

Pasta has been made in Italy as far back as Roman times.

In Bologna I was taught how to make delicious egg pasta by Mamma Adriana.

Then we enjoyed eating a real Spaghetti Bolognese at a local restaurant.

13

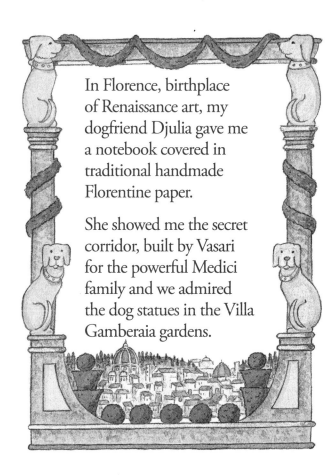

In Florence, birthplace of Renaissance art, my dogfriend Djulia gave me a notebook covered in traditional handmade Florentine paper.

She showed me the secret corridor, built by Vasari for the powerful Medici family and we admired the dog statues in the Villa Gamberaia gardens.

Pisa is built on reclaimed land. Some years ago, the medieval tower was leaning so dangerously that it nearly fell down.

Galileo, the great astronomer of the Renaissance, who discovered the planets orbit the sun, was born in Pisa.

My elegant friend Eugenio
took me to San Gimignano,
often called the Manhattan
of Tuscany because of its
high towers.

In medieval times, there
were 72 of these built by
the wealthiest families.
14 of the towers are
still standing.

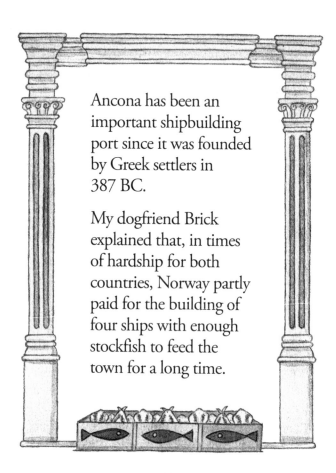

Ancona has been an important shipbuilding port since it was founded by Greek settlers in 387 BC.

My dogfriend Brick explained that, in times of hardship for both countries, Norway partly paid for the building of four ships with enough stockfish to feed the town for a long time.

I was taught to make Baci kisses by chocolate master Massimiliano of Perugia.

Then I visited my many Umbrian Labrador cousins.

Although real chocolate is poisonous to dogs I enjoyed lots of doggy kisses from Chocolate Labrador Merlin.

In Rome I met my dogfriend Claudio. We rode his Vespa around the Colosseum and all the city sights.

I threw a coin into the Trevi Fountain to make sure I would return to Rome. It was very hot so we jumped in!

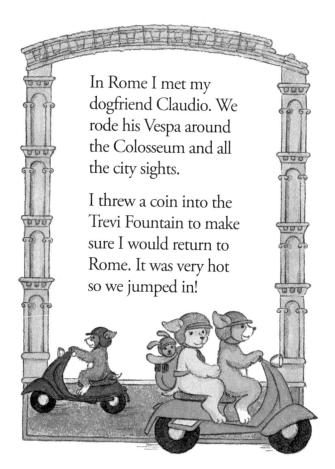

The dome of St Peter's Basilica in the Vatican, one of the most renowned works of Renaissance architecture, was designed by Michelangelo who also painted the ceiling of the Sistine Chapel.

I visited Monsignor Andreatti in his rooftop garden where we picked lemons together.

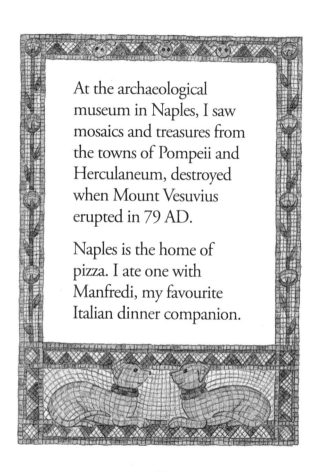

At the archaeological museum in Naples, I saw mosaics and treasures from the towns of Pompeii and Herculaneum, destroyed when Mount Vesuvius erupted in 79 AD.

Naples is the home of pizza. I ate one with Manfredi, my favourite Italian dinner companion.

I bought Italian gifts for my family at Highclere Castle. Masks from Venice, a bottle of Limoncello for Mummy Bella and, of course, some of his favorite salami sausage for Grandpup.

Goodbye Italy!
Ciao Italia!

DOGOLOGY

Finse met some old dear friends in Italy and made many fine new ones.